Rock, Paper,

ALSO BY RICHARD OSMOND

Useful Verses

Richard Osmond

Rock, Paper, Scissors

PICADOR

First published 2019 by Picador
an imprint of Pan Macmillan
20 New Wharf Road, London N1 9RR
Associated companies throughout the world
www.panmacmillan.com

ISBN 978-1-5098-9458-1

1 3 5 7 9 8 6 4 2

A CIP catalogue record for this book is available from the British Library.

Printed and bound by CPI Group (UK) Ltd, Croydon, CR0 4YY

Visit **www.picador.com** to read more about all our books
and to buy them. You will also find features, author interviews and
news of any author events, and you can sign up for e-newsletters
so that you're always first to hear about our new releases.

This book is dedicated to the memory of
Christine Archibald
James McMullan
Kirsty Boden
Sara Zelenak
Alexandre Pigeard
Sebastien Belanger
Xavier Thomas
Ignacio Echeverría

Contents

Author's Note

On June 3rd 2017 I was out drinking with friends in the Borough Market area of London when a van was deliberately driven into pedestrians on London Bridge. Its three occupants got out, ran to Borough Market and began stabbing people in and around the restaurants and pubs in that area. They were then shot by police. This book is a response to being caught up in the incident. Rather than documenting the events themselves, it documents my attempts to make sense of my experiences or, more often than not, to explore the ways in which they *don't* make sense.

The poems in *Rock, Paper, Scissors* fall into three main categories: my translations of excerpts from *Beowulf*, with a close focus on Grendel's attacks on Heorot; a selection of my own translations of mostly short verses from the Qur'ān; original poems from my own point of view, mostly relating to my experiences on the night of June 3rd.

A book like this has the potential to be quite controversial in terms of both its subject matter and in some of its sources and strategies. With this in mind, I have included, after the poems, some brief discussions of my methods and intentions, aiming to elucidate my approach to the work and the reasons for selecting the source texts I did. I hope these, as well as the poems themselves, will speak for my sincerity when I say that the book is a personal response to a personal experience, and as such does not come with a moral or political agenda, nor any intention to offend, inflame, appropriate or stereotype.

I've also made an effort to document and justify any linguistic liberties I've taken – with the Qur'ān in particular, but with the Old English too – in line-specific translator's notes, offering insight into any unusual word choices or unconventional renderings. These immediately follow the longer explanatory passages at the end of the book.

Richard Osmond

Rock, Paper, Scissors

The Creation Song

Beowulf 86–102

The brazen ghoul who dwelled in the dark
had a hard time, having to hear
each and every day the loud sound
of people having fun in the hall:

There was the harp's clear ringing.
There was sweet song sung by a singer
who, since he knew how to sing so well
of mankind's making long ago, did so:

The singer said the Almighty made the earth –
all aspects and elevations of those
bright meadows about which water bows
and bends – and held the sun

and moon aloft like gleaming trophies
and covered all the corners of the earth
with a decorative fretwork of boughs,
branches, limbs & leaves. He shaped or sang

every moving kind of thing alive to life.
And so the lord's men lived the dream
until someone (a murdering fiend,
a wendigo, a demon from the depths of hell)

began to commit atrocities.
His name was Grendel.

The Bee

Qur'ān 16. 66–69

A sign will be apparent here to those
who reason. God inspires the bee
directly: 'Bee, build in the mountains,
build in trees and houses, build in buildings.

Feed on all fruits and follow
in the paths and holloways
trodden for you by the Lord,'
and from the bee's belly flows

a drink of many colours
to feed and heal mankind.
Surely, on reflection,
this must be a sign.

Sand

I'm on the beach in Galveston with Beth's son Luke,
who is four. We build a castle, then we build a turtle
and a tunafish chasing the turtle and a whale
about to swallow the tunafish and turtle
and then Luke builds a car crashing into the whale.
Stories told in sand are clearly not
beholden to the classical unities, nor obliged
to be consistently either comic or serious in tone;
anything can collide with anything else at any time,
as in life. Herring gulls want to eat our Cheez-Its.
A van ploughs into pedestrians on London Bridge.
I use a piece of string to give the turtle a silly smile.
Luke laughs at this. Someone pulls a grey blanket
over a man in Borough Market.

I come with a sign from God

Qur'ān 3. 49

I make for you from clay
the shape of a bird and breathe
into it and it becomes
a bird.

Grendel came creeping out,

Beowulf 710–720

under cover of fog
carrying the full weight of the wrath of God
on his shoulders. Grendel:

a reaper with a mind to grab a handful
of mankind.
             Through mist,
he saw the beer hall lit in bright gold
before him. This wasn't the first time
he had found his way to Hrothgar's house,
but he had never met
such tough luck or tough men.
Such hard luck or hard men.

The doors, despite being
twice reinforced,
double-barred hard
with iron rebar,
burst open at the touch
of the grim one's
bad-intentioned hands
when he tore in fury
at the mead hall's mouth.

Rock, Paper, Scissors

Eight hours into Rob's stag, which had
started strong with a pub crawl up
the Bermondsey beer mile
and was now beginning to sag
at a Wetherspoon's near Tower Bridge,
a match of rock, paper, scissors
was breaking out to pick between
the following two options
for what would happen next:

1: We go to Katzenjammers
authentic German bierkeller
under London Bridge, where we would
listen to an oompah band, eat sauerkraut,
drink litre steins of Paulaner Dunkel
and be held in the basement
by police for our own protection
as terrorists attacked the door outside,
see bloody victims hurry down
the stairs to shelter in the bar,
watch paramedics treat
slash wounds to the throat and
stab wounds to the stomach, and
slash and stab wounds
to the throat and stomach and
hear a woman sob and hyperventilate
because of what she couldn't

bring herself to tell us she had seen
up on street level
and take cover under
the traditional wooden benches
when armed officers burst in
with automatic weapons
yelling, 'Down, Get down! GET. DOWN.'

or 2: We go to a strip club.

The game began, Emmett and Matt
competing. *So it's 'One, two, three, Go'*
and play on Go. One, two, three, Go.
Both guys threw down scissors first.
One, two, three, Go.
Both changed tack dramatically
and went for paper –
all bets were off.
One, two, three, Go.
They cast their final shapes.
Emmett, for the bier bar,
stuck fatefully with paper
while Matt, solidly in favour
of the strip club,
chose rock and lost.
The decision had been made

and I dwell on it for bathos, mainly,
and because the world is made of games
of rock, paper, scissors like this one.

[7]

Not only in the sense that every flip
or arbitrary choice has disproportionately
huge and permanent results
but in the sense that every gesture,
either of victory or defeat,
aggression or surrender,
depends for its meaning on another.

Put it this way: a photograph
of Matt's third and losing move,
viewed in isolation, appears
to show a man raising his fist in anger,
about to throw a punch. Only those who know
which game of signs he's playing at
will read the hand as *rock*.
And even *rock* means nothing
without further context:
in rock, paper, scissors, *rock*
is capable of meaning strength
or weakness or indifference
depending on the sign
selected to contest it.

We called an Uber to take us to London Bridge.

The Mosquito

Qur'ān 2. 26

God is not averse to parables. For example
he might use the mosquito as an analogy.

All those who believe will understand
this analogy and know it to be true.

Those who do not believe will say,
'What point is He trying to make?'

Thus, God guides some
and lets others go astray.

The Work of Satan

Qur'ān, Al-Maeda 5. 90

Seriously,
alcohol and games of chance –
drinking booze and using darts
to tell the future – intoxicating liquors
and animal sacrifice at the altar –
these are the work of Satan
and must be avoided.

Hrothgar speaks I

Beowulf 480–483

Having drunk beer, men make promises
somewhere between idle boast
and solemn oath – words which must
be honoured all the more
for having been sworn half-cut:
the battle-blokes bet each other
over beers that they would stay put
and await the attack, knives out.

Do not be weak

(3 versions)

Qur'ān 4. 104

Do not lose heart in hunting them.
They hurt as you hurt,
but you expect what they do not
from Allah.

/

Do not lessen your efforts to find and fight
the unbelievers. They have the same capacity
to feel pain as you do, but you foresee
and believe in something they do not
(an afterlife: God's promise of paradise).

/

Do not be weak in pursuing
people. If you are

suffering, then they are
suffering as you are
suffering,

but you
have hope
for that
from God
for which

they have no hope.

Get Down

Every emergency exit
opens onto stairs which lead
up to different streets.

So when a squad securing the area
wants to disappear strategically
from one street corner on the surface
and re-appear on another
they come down one set of stairs,
cross our basement bar where
hundreds of people full of lager
are confined and exit up another.

And every time they pass through the crowd
we have to get down on the floor again.
The second time it happens,
an armed officer shouts, 'Get on the floor.'
A group of us get down on the floor
with our backs against the bar.
He shouts 'Lower' but we're already on the floor
so all we can do is sort of go limp
and slide down further so we're lying
like ragdolls with only our heads propped up
at unnatural angles against the bar
and walls and each other's legs
and watch as a group of people
get stuck between the police
and their intended exit.

Because of the crush
and because they're drunk
they don't get out of the way
or down fast enough and things
get tense and people shout at them
and they shout back and the lead officer
doesn't exactly point his gun
but his grip on it does tighten.

He yells, 'Get down,' again,
but desperate now: He's not saying,
'Get down because I have a gun
and I will shoot you if you don't'
but 'Get down because I have a gun
and that means nothing in this situation'.
'Get down because actually to use a gun
is to lose the authority it commands:
if you, the hundreds of people in this room
loaded past its safe capacity, refused
to get down then what would I do?
Shoot each and every one of you?
If one person tried to grab the gun,
what would I do? Shoot them?
As if I could even choose
who to shoot and not to shoot.
In a space like this I might as well
just shut my eyes and pull the trigger
and let the bullet ricochet –
GET. DOWN.'

Do the unbelievers not consider the Qur'ān?

Qur'ān 4. 82

Surely if the Qur'ān came from anywhere
other than straight from God himself,
it would be full of contradictions.

Osama Bin Grendel

Long before the terrorists at London Bridge adopted
the dread troll Grendel's modus operandi,
bursting by night into beer halls,
where mankind sat drinking ale,
and slashing throats,

I jotted the beginnings of a joke
in the back of my Anglo-Saxon textbook:
'Reasons why Grendel
from *Beowulf* and Osama Bin Laden are
secretly the same person.' Stuff like:

Both were resentful outsiders
who attacked a social order
founded on and fortified by
the exchange of riches.

Both of their attacks were focused on
a large building which was at once
a symbolic focal point of this social order
and the actual location where the
riches were exchanged.

Both of them hid in a cave.

And you never see the two of them
in the same room together, do you?

When reading this aloud and no one laughs
I tell myself that the clearing of throats
and the sound of chair legs scraping on the floor
can actually be said to amplify the poem's
deliberately uncomfortable and dissonant effects.

Hrothgar speaks II

Beowulf 484–490

The morning after the attack, the mead hall
was gore-splattered: dawn revealed
the long benches smeared with blood.
I was a few brave friends the fewer.

Sit down to eat, men.
Obey your hearts: uncork
your thoughts and talk
about our brave soldiers
and their glory in war.

Image

A nude faux-leather
woman's high heeled shoe,
lying on its side.

An allegory for His light is

Qur'ān 24. 35

an alcove.
In the alcove is set a lamp.
The lamp is in a glass.
The glass is a shining planet
fuelled by a tree:
a blessed olive neither
of the West nor East
the oil of which is of such
a quality that it seems

to glow before the fire
has touched it.
Light upon light.

There's no signal

I'm trying to get a hold of Jenny,
who is still in Texas for a few
more days, to let her know I'm safe.

Her friends Beth and Tyler live
in Dickinson, Galveston county, but
are considering a move to Michigan;

Tyler is a firefighter and Detroit
offers greater opportunities.
They have more fires there, he says.

Thunder

Qur'ān 2. 19–20

A storm breaks from above,
full of darkness and thunder
and lightning. The unbelievers
stick their fingers in their ears
against the thunderclaps
for fear of death
as God surrounds them.

The lightning nearly takes their sight.
They walk only when it flashes
to illuminate the way
but stand still in the dark.

There's still no signal —

Only one app loads and works;
it sends me a notification:

At sixteen weeks your baby is now
the size of an avocado. She can move

all of her joints and limbs.
She can sense light

though her eyelids are fused shut.

Abandoned notes towards a poem
for Alexandre Pigeard

'Alexandre Pigeard was passionate
about electronic music, a member
of the Club 808 collective'
            From a statement by Alexandre Pigeard's family

I found his music still online,
started to write something
  in memoriam and immediately
  felt guilty and exploitative
    for Googling so detachedly and
    for thinking to invoke him
      and others in my book
      as though I had any right to speak
        and write about or for
        the dead and those who suffered and
    for hoping his presence in these pages might
      lend the poems more legitimacy
        as though my own peripheral
          experience could be anointed
          truer by his blood
so I stopped. But that night

I opened my computer in the dark
downstairs and a Pigeard house mix started
playing from his soundcloud.

For a split, I heard
the track outside the context
of a key or cadence.
I heard

his music as it was, or as a startled pigeon might /
    a mouse, simple
        and afraid enough
        to hear the world
        as noise un-patterned
        by all but its most
        present dangers.

Contemplate the paradox:
    electronic dance
    played to no one in an empty room
    by a DJ who is dead,
    stabbed in the neck by terrorists.

It doesn't work. Without euphoric bodies dancing to the synth that
builds before the drop, the synth that builds before the drop is
torturous – the sound of a city's whole machinery in unresolvable
panic. Without a beating heart to beat in counterpoint to the beat
or a brain alive to count the beat in measures, each bass kick
becomes the blank totality of death itself experienced endlessly as
one terrible instant

Sick Flame

Beowulf 720–745

The evil one advanced angrily

over the beer hall's flagstone floor.
His eyes fixed (and in them a sick
flame flickered) on a band of men
sleeping there together

and his heart leapt at the thought
    of tearing each man life from limb

and his heart leapt at the thought
    of severing each man's soul
        from his body, one by one.

He foresaw for himself a feast
of human meat that night
and he was right, but fate had it
that the feast would be his last.

The beast didn't delay.
He took the first opportunity
to seize, slash and slay
a sleeping man.
He bit into the sinews

which bound his bones together.
He drank the blood and gulped down
great gobs of flesh.

Soon he had swallowed
the whole dead man,
even his feet and hands.

A tall thin man

I didn't see him in that imagistic way a poet in a poem
sees things like a wheelbarrow or a discarded woman's shoe
and captures them and their whole essence out of time.

I saw him, lost him in the crowd, found him, looked away
and then looked back again to check that what I saw was
what I thought it was. It was:

A tall thin man.
A tall thin man holding bundled cloth against his neck.
A tall thin man with wadded fabric held against his neck soaked
with blood-red blood who had found his way downstairs to
Katzenjammers to shelter underground with an expression on his
face I didn't recognise at first because, just as I did not perceive
him in a singular or poetic way, neither did he perform his
suffering according to convention but looked frightened in a way
few actors would act when asked to portray fear: blank,
withdrawn and with a gait and posture of both stiff dignity and
urgent shame. Like one of those people you read about who, when
they start to choke in public, hurry to the bathroom in
embarrassment and die alone.

And as for poets,

Qur'ān, 26. 223

deviants follow them.

Haven't you noticed them
roaming the valleys

saying the opposite of what they do?

If all the trees on earth were pens

Qur'ān, 31. 27

and the sea were ink
and if, when the sea ran out,
the trees could be refilled
with seven more seas of ink the same

to write the word of God,
the word of God
would never be used up.

On Memory

In many ways, I know fewer of the facts
of June 3rd than those who watched it on the news
or followed it on Twitter since a) we spent most
of the incident crouching underground with no data
service being told to do nothing and go nowhere
and b) the vividness of a memory is not
necessarily commensurate with its gravity
or consequence. For example:

I had just slid off the wooden bench again
to keep my head low while making way
for the police to pass on their third or fourth
armed crossing of the bar when in the trembling
silence an ethereal smoke or vapour billowed
from a nearby bench. Looking down I saw
it was Rob's mate Dan from the brewery
hunched and hugging his knees like a chimp
to fit under the table and sucking on a vape pen.
He gave me a shrug and comic wide-eyed look
which somehow managed to communicate at once
both real fear and self-aware awkwardness
before I lost his face again behind the thick
white cherry-scented haze of water
and propylene glycol.

Fighting

Qur'ān, 2. 216

Fighting is prescribed to you,
even though you hate it.

Maybe you dislike something which is good for you.
Maybe you love something which is bad for you.

God knows.
You do not know.

Life

Qur'ān, 6. 32

It's nothing – life in this world –
but play and diversion. Fun and games.

The Three

Rock, paper, scissors
originated in Japan as *sansukumi-ken*
or *fist-game of the three*
who are afraid of one another.

Grip

Beowulf 749–765

He *(who?)*
the warrior *(which?)*
the one in whose wake incidents
of outrageous cruelty flocked and followed
like sheep behind a shepherd,
found that he was now encountering a grip
the match of the strength of which

he had never met before
in the hand of any man in any of
the nooks, fjords or four corners
of this wide world of men. In his

mind
he grew scared in his
soul
and afraid at
heart.

He couldn't flee fast enough.
He wanted to escape into the dark and run
to where the devils are.

His life at this moment was unlike
his life had ever been before.

The good man *(Beowulf)* bore
in mind what had been said that night and stood
uplong and grabbed and held him
firm and fast. His fingers fell off.
(Whose fingers fell off?)
His fingers fell off.

The monster twisted or tried to twist
and turn back outward and away
but the man stepped up.

The infamous fiend's intention was to find
any exit or escape he could and then
to fly into his hollow fen and hide,
and if doing so meant he'd have to lose
his fingers in a foe's grip, as he knew he would,
he would.

The Elephant

Qur'ān 105. 1–5

Don't you know
how your Lord dealt
with the elephant handlers?

How he foiled their plan?

He sent great flocks of birds
to pelt them from above
with rocks of hard-baked clay.

He left them as hollow,
torn and shredded
as macerated straw.

Of Horror

Although I find Žižek pretty insufferable
he is right to say, in *The Pervert's Guide to Cinema*,
that the fantastical or monstrous elements of horror
often feel like stains on reality – strange blemishes
superimposed onto or cut into the narrative
so as to manifest its unspoken tensions,
e.g.

Hitchcock's birds arrive with no more sense
of motive or distinctiveness of meaning
than if someone had accidentally splattered
white paint on the lens; they are aberrations
on the surface of an uncomfortable story
about a mother's power over and taboo desire for
her own son. Terrible gulls turn unspeakable things
like incest into tangible forms

as do signifiers in Freud's conception of the dream.
Elevator doors open to release a tidal wash of gore
into a hotel corridor. An alien abomination of tentacles
and teeth bursts bloody from a man's stomach.
A night of revelry is interrupted by a blood-drinking
flesh-eating troll.

As more of the wounded stumbled down
the stairs in search of help, I thought
of those iconic scenes – the unexpected

but inevitable intrusion into and return to life
of all that we repress, expressed in blood:
too much blood or blood where there shouldn't be blood.

Rumour

Qur'ān 4. 83

When a situation arises
relating to security or fear
they spread it as a rumour,
even though referring it
to the proper authorities
would result in it being
dealt with by those better
equipped to make correct
decisions.

Black Friday

Panicked shoppers flee Oxford Street
after reports claim 'shots fired'
Panic on London's Oxford Street
after reports of shooting
Oxford Street 'shooting': Police
scramble to 'shots fired'
Oxford Circus: police stood down
after incident in central London – as
Oxford Circus Tube station:
Pair sought over platform altercation
Oxford Street panic as shoppers
'run and scream' after false reports of . . .
'No shots, no casualties'
after panic at Oxford Circus
Oxford Street: What happened? All we know
so far about the incident . . .
Oxford Circus: Terror alert on London's
busiest shopping street . . .
Oxford Circus terror scare: Nine people
rushed to hospital as false . . .
Oxford Street panic: Woman hurt
after 'shots fired' false alarm
Oxford Street panic began with fight
at tube station, suggest police . . .
Oxford Circus: police stood down
after incident in central London – as . . .

False alarm sparks panic on
London's Oxford Street

The prologue to Shakespeare's *Henry IV part II* is spoken
by the abstract concept of *Rumour* personified as a man,
his robes 'painted full of tongues'.

Singer Olly Murs tweets the terror in London
as Oxford Circus false alarm sparks panic.
Singer Olly Murs describes the terror in London
as Oxford Circus false . . .
Olly Murs' shocking tweets as Oxford Street
incident unfolds
Olly Murs defends 'fake news' tweets after claiming
he heard 'gunshots' in Selfridges
Police find no evidence of shots
fired at Oxford Circus

Fuck everyone get out of @Selfridges now gun shots!! I'm inside

Magnitude

Alarmed tweets travel forty thousand
times faster than seismic waves from
their original fault: the quake is trending
long before you feel it.

The Zaqqum Tree I

Qur'ān 37. 62

The Zaqqum Tree is a tree
which grows from the very bottom
of the inferno – from the fiery roots of hell.

The conspicuous bracts surrounding
or subtending its ripening fruit
are like the wicked heads of devils

and those who have done wrong must eat
and fill their bellies with this fruit,
washed down with a brew of boiling water.

Tense

We took the Jubilee eastward at Southwark and
a taxi back from North Greenwich to Rob's.
BBC News was already looping iPhone footage
clearly shot from the same corner of the same
bar we'd been crouching in an hour before. Under
the video a ribbon of text crawled by in that
indefinite present tense which makes headlines
sound less like unfolding incidents which have
just now occurred and more like universal axioms
describing the typical behaviour of things:

TERROR ATTACKS THE HEART OF LONDON
PEDESTRIANS FLEE A VAN ON LONDON BRIDGE
MEN ATTACK LONDONERS WITH HUNTING KNIVES
POLICE SHOOT ATTACKERS DEAD

burston banlocan

Beowulf 805–823

His unwilling severance from his own
accumulated age – the end of his stretch
of days spent alive – would be wretched.

On that night of his life (his last)
this weird spirit,
the ghost of an alien,
would fare forth far into places
administered and ruled over
by fiends.

He
who had committed so many crimes
against mankind with misery and murder in mind,
he
who was in a perpetual state of feud with God,
he
knew his body wouldn't last.

Hygelac's heir, in a brave
mood – moody in a brave way –
brave in both mood and mind –
had him by the hand with his hand.

Each one was by the other
loathed in life.
A lifelong loathing.
Each was loath for the other to live.

The fierce monster, the deadly warrior
was hurt in corpse. Litch-sore. A great wound grew
on his shoulder. Sinews un-sprung;
the bone-locks which locked his bones closed
burst open and all his cords and connective tissues
un-coupled one by one

and the glory went to Beowulf.

Grendel had to flee, life-force-failing,
to the fen's foothills and down deeper
underneath the marshes,
to find and hide in his unhappy home
where he knew his days' end had come:
the daily countdown of his life's days was done.

Live

The next day two television channels
invited me to describe my experience on the news,
on the condition, in both cases, that I return
to the scene to be interviewed in front of the
cordoned-off stretch of London Bridge where
the van had swerved the night before, up the road
from where three men were shot, round the corner
from where an officer in a Hi-Vis jacket finally
let us out of the cellar bar's emergency exit and
onto Southwark Street, heading west, and said,
    When I tell you to go, just keep going that way,
    go quickly and don't stop. Just keep walking.
    Don't come back. Go now, keep going. Run.
    and we broke into a run.

The Zaqqum Tree II

Qur'ān 44. 43–59

The tree of bitterness.
Sinner-food. Its fruit
will bubble in the belly like molten metal –
seethe and simmer like scalding water.

Seize him and take him
to the heart of fire!
Pour boiling liquid punishment
over his head!

You, the once-powerful,
the once-refined and dignified,
this is precisely what you
didn't believe would happen.

And all the while the righteous
will be safe in gardens
next to freshwater springs
dressed in outfits of both light
and heavy shuttle-woven silk,
charmeuse and brocade,
sitting face to face
with each other.

They'll be married
to beautiful people
with beautiful eyes
like freshwater springs,
and be free
to call for any kind of fruit they like.

Poetry

In October 2018 I was interviewed
about this book on *ITV London News*.
As I answered questions on the nature
of poetry as a response to traumatic
experience my voice was layered
over silent images of that night

or rather images of police, paramedics
and the luminous cordons they erect
to keep the media at a safe remove
from the matter of their work.

The interview, which appeared
to take place in an industrial-chic
studio environment – all exposed wood,
glass and steel, a panorama of the city
skyline to the rear – was actually shot
in a windowless basement painted
uniformly green, the colour
of the leaves of fragrant butterbur
or winter heliotrope, a bright
but natural hue which chromakey
technology in the vision mixer
made transparent and replaced
with images of the non-existent set.

While citing some of the online resources
my translations drew upon, I have
discovered that one website,
corpus.quran.com, is not only a
tool to help readers parse the intricate
grammar of the Qur'ān: it is an exercise
in computational and corpus linguistics,
combining morphological and syntactic
annotations with a complex branching
diagram of the ontology of concepts
within the text for the express purpose
of one day creating, out of the verbatim
and unaltered word of Allah as revealed
to the Prophet Muhammad through the
Archangel Gabriel, an artificial intelligence
entirely fluent in Qur'ānic Arabic, capable
of directly conversing with students about
the spiritual message of the book with
no intervention from the programmer
who created it.

earm ond eaxl

Beowulf 833–836

When war-bold Beowulf placed
the entirety of Grendel's grip –

his whole torn-off shoulder –
his whole arm and hand together –

on display beneath
the big hole in the hall roof,
the sign was unambiguous.

Notes

Beowulf

It will be obvious why I have chosen this particular episode of *Beowulf* – Grendel's attacks on the beer hall, Heorot – for inclusion in the book: the similarities between the events of June 3rd and the events depicted in the Old English poem are striking. *Beowulf* is also my favourite long poem – the one I know best and re-read the most often. Soon after the attack, when I was confused and shaken and needed personally to process what had happened, it felt natural to write the events through *Beowulf*. It is, for me, a text so enigmatic and full of frightening mystery that it seemed some-how to encode aspects of the inexplicable experience I was dealing with.

In my translations, I've tried to avoid gimmicky bias towards modern lexicons and registers such as those relating to terrorism, law enforcement, modern weaponry and so on. Where I had a free choice in how to render a word, I selected modern English words based on what best communicated the sense and feeling of the original text and, to be honest, what I found most stimulating and interesting. (The more detailed notes on individual poems provide justification for some of the unusual choices I made.) As a result, the surprising echoes of modern events found throughout these excerpts are largely there because they are present in the original. Or perhaps because we haven't come all that far in a thousand years.

The Qur'ān

My publishers and I thought it best that I clarify my intention in using the Qur'ān. Of course, it's hard to pin down anyone's intention at the best of times. The truth is that when I made this book I wrote instinctively, following whatever felt important or interesting or personally useful in putting feeling into words. I certainly didn't approach the project with the intention of making any kind of judgement, ethical statement or political call to action. The work was my personal response to what happened – a record of my working-through of a troubling experience. So, the reasoning below is less a description of my explicit intention at the time, or of my overriding scheme or plan for the book (I had none), than a retrospective attempt to identify precisely what it was about the Qur'ān which made me choose it and use it in the way I did. These three reasons feel most important:

1: What happened on June 3rd was unprecedented in my life experience. In writing about the event, I wanted to express my feeling that the events were not categorisable by any of the terms which define everyday experience and that they were resistant to being represented by any of my usual poetic practice. One reason I was drawn towards the Qur'ān was that its special cultural position reminded me of the peculiar transcendence I was looking for. In terms of its significance and status, the Qur'ān inhabits a different category of text and meaning from any book I can think of, even the foundational texts of other religions. If part of that transcendence and special quality was an aura of sacrosanctity and unassailability which made me feel very wary and nervous about translating it and using it in my work, so much the better: this perfectly matched the wary nervousness I was already experiencing about the project as a whole.

2: As well as its transcendent, holy status in Islam, the Qur'ān is further separated and made unique among books by the controversy which swirls around it. It is hard to approach the Qur'ān as a white British poet without becoming caught up in the political and social debates surrounding Islam, multiculturalism, Muslims in Britain, Islamophobia in British nationalist thinking, fundamentalism, terrorism and 'Islamic State'. All these topics felt as frightening, crucial and taboo as the violence, injury and terror I had witnessed and intended to write about. There was a heat and controversy to the idea of translating from this book which felt appropriate to the project: firstly because, as a subject for poetry, my experiences of June 3rd felt unusually immediate, current and risky – in short suffused with a similar intensity and danger to the debates and controversies itemised above. Secondly because the events of June 3rd, in both origin and consequence, were themselves part of these very debates and controversies.

3: Since I've just acknowledged that 'heat and controversy' were part of the Qur'ān's draw for me, I can hardly complain if, as a white British poet re-contextualising the Qur'ān for my own purposes, I am accused of insensitivity or appropriation. But I fear I might be. I hope this last reason will go some way to answering such concerns:

Quite contrarily to the negative stereotype of Islam as being monolithic, proscriptive and single-minded in its judgements, while working on this book I have found the Qur'ān to be astonishingly enigmatic, ambivalent, even gnomic. As *Rock, Paper, Scissors* developed into a book concerned with the making of meaning from events, experiences and texts which are paradoxical, fragmented and complex, the Qur'ānic excerpts became more and more central to the writing process. This book became a book about the potential hazards of re-making meaning from difficult texts in difficult contexts.

Sections of the Qur'ān, taken out of context, are used to fuel the rhetorical fires of hate and fear at both extremes of the discourse – anti-Muslim British nationalist bigots on one side and ISIS fundamentalist death-cultists on the other. I hope it will be clear, when reading *Rock, Paper, Scissors*, that I'm trying to forefront the text itself and, in so doing, show the almost comically wide gap between, on one hand, the Qur'ān's incredible diversity of thought, ambivalence of philosophy and vividness of colour and, on the other, the singular dogmatism of those on every side of the ideological debate who purport to have read it.

Original Poems

My own narrative does not seek fully to report or recount the events of June 3rd.

Eight innocent people died that night, with dozens more injured. The three attackers were shot dead. I am in no way qualified or entitled to speak for the dead or their families, nor to attempt to make art from the suffering of others. For me to claim these poems are anything other than a personal response to a personal experience would be to claim ownership and authority over something to which I have no right. Limiting myself to such a response has produced a book that I hope is honest, but is certainly not pretending to be definitive. The book could never hope to honour the memory of those innocent people who lost their lives on June 3rd 2017. Nonetheless, it is dedicated to them:

Christine Archibald

James McMullan

Kirsty Boden

Sara Zelenak

Alexandre Pigeard

Sebastien Belanger

Xavier Thomas

Ignacio Echeverría

R O

Notes on Translations

The Creation Song

l.13 This is my attempt to reflect some of the sense of the word 'sigehreþig', used in the original to describe the sun and the moon. Literally it means 'victory-famed' or 'success-glorious'. In Old English poetry, references to the glories of battle-triumph are go-to descriptors, seemingly used to describe almost everything, whereas in modern English a bit of extra mental legwork is necessary to get full value from the connection between the shining of the sun and the glory of winning.

l.15 The original word is 'gefrætwade', which means decorated / ornamented. I used 'fretwork' because of the etymological connection between the two words, and also because the designs of traditional fretwork have something of the organic, intertwining intricacy that Old English poetry, jewellery and art seem to value.

l.16 That the poet/singer here is competing subtly with the Almighty to be the main subject of the verse is intentional and, I think, present in the original. There is a conceptual exchange between their two actions – the singer performs the act of creation with his composition and performance; the Almighty Creator sings the world to life like a song.

l.18 This is an attempt to preserve a piece of the original language, perhaps at the expense of good translation. The word 'dream' is also used in the original Old English, but it's a false friend – it actually means 'joy'. But I can't help reading it with a hint of the modern sense of 'dream'. So with 'living the dream' I've tried to find an idiom which means 'joy and happiness' but nonetheless uses the word dream.

The Bee
1.6 'holloways' takes a liberty. The original has the plainer sense of God having pre-ordained and pre-trodden paths for the bee. Holloways are specifically those ancient English roads and paths worn into the earth by thousands of years of traffic, often made into perfect shady tunnels by the trees which grow overhead. There was something appealing about this because of some associations I haven't quite made explicit even to myself. The holloway made me think of the concept of 'desire paths' in human spaces, which in turn made me think of the study of the behaviour of bees individually and in hives. Since the beehive is partly being invoked here as a figure for human society, I allowed the translation to follow my drift.

Grendel came creeping out
l.17 Old English is a language which tolerates, especially in its poetry, much more repetition than is natural in modern English. There are times when I've decided this repetition is an unnecessary feature, but others, like this one, where the repetition seems crucial, and serves more of a purpose than plain emphasis: here, the re-inforcement of the door is reinforced by repetitious language in the original. This represents one of several techniques I've tried out in this book to represent Old English repetition without making the poem sound like a broken record.

Hrothgar speaks I
l.3 Some words in *Beowulf* would have carried a weight and cultural significance to their original audience which is never made totally explicit and can sometimes be lost in modern translation. My trans-lation of this sentence represents an attempt to make some of the poem's cultural context and social subtext as available to readers now as it might have been to readers then. Promises made while drunk, in this culture, which placed so much ceremonial import-ance on ale-sharing, were worth more, not less, than promises made while sober. The original passage is much simpler – literally it says something like, 'Very often battle-men have vowed over ale-cups, drunk on beer'.

Do not be weak
l.15 Parsing a case-inflected language, with its free word-ordering, and rendering it into idiomatic modern English can be painstaking. With this stack of nouns and pronouns (and their nested dative relationships) I have tried to preserve some of the difficulty and flavour of reading the original.

Sick Flame

l.7 To repeat this line is my decision. The original uses the Old English poetic technique of apposition to replay the same actions multiple times, one by one, with different verbs and descriptions. By repeating this line so identically, I'm trying to give the original's repetition the emphasis and urgency it needs to feel justified in modern English.

Life

l.2 This isn't so repetitive in the original. Were it to appear on its own, I think the very English-sounding 'fun and games' would make readers curious about the literal sense of the original. I've pre-empted this by translating the original phrase twice in the hope of finding meaning somewhere between the two alternatives.

Grip

ll. 1–2 The original purposely blurs the distinction between Grendel and Beowulf. See notes below on l.25 of *burston banlocan* for more details. For me, one thrill of reading the original has always been that the characters move too fast to keep track of. By adding the confused call-and-response interjections/annotations which appear throughout this excerpt, I'm attempting to embody both the frenetic, disorientating effects of the original, and the one-two punch rhythms of Anglo-Saxon alliterative half-lines at their most energetic.

l.3 In the original, this long sheep-trope is just a two-word descriptor attached to Grendel: 'fyrena hyrde', which means 'shepherd of atrocities'. This is such an interesting description that I decided to unpack it into a more traditionally-expressed simile.

l.24 'Uplong' is a word I've ported directly from the original. It means precisely what you'd expect it to mean. I'm hereby claiming it for modern English.

The Elephant

ll.8–10 This final image is expanded a little from the original, which would be more accurately translated as 'He left them like eaten straw.' But what are the qualities of eaten straw? Phrased so concisely, it sounds almost like a riddle. My version attempts to fill in the image with some more specific description and agriculture, inspired by my local cattle farmer, who gives macerated straw to his cows in the winter, mixed with warm molasses.

The Zaqqum Tree I

l.5 The whole of this line and the line before it is my liberal translation of a single Arabic word which is usually just translated as 'fruit'. What I found interesting personally (as a poet/forager interested in the way botanical vocabulary can behave in poems) is that it literally means 'spathe / spadix' – the outer husk of the fruit of certain palm trees. The use of such a word probably sounds overly technical and taxonomical to speakers of modern English and residents of the British Isles, but to a culture which evolved among fresh-grown dates and a variety of other palms, this must be a much more everyday word-and-thing without the specificity of register 'spadix' has in English. As an experiment, or a treat for myself, really, I played up this disjunction between common and botanical usage by quoting verbatim a dictionary definition of 'spadix' here, where 'fruit' alone would have easily sufficed.

burston banlocan

l.3 I've leaned on the repetition of *life* here to set up how the passage becomes preoccupied with the idea of how we conceive of our life and its ending. Also, it's an attempt to explore the nuances and differing connotations between the two Old English words for life used in this passage – 'aldor' and 'lif'.

l.25 I have translated one phrase twice here. Old English uses a word, 'æglæca', which is applied at different times to both Beowulf and Grendel. Generally when describing Grendel it is rendered as 'monster', 'troll', 'beast'. When given to Beowulf it is translated as 'warrior', 'fighter' etc. But clearly this leads to some overlap and blurring – Grendel's fighting skill is so great that the monster starts to resemble a fierce and honourable warrior. Beowulf's fearsome war-prowess is so great that the warrior prince becomes faintly monstrous. And, as will be obvious from the fight scenes presented in this book, when the two face off against each other there tends to be some confusion about who is whom, with the individual identities of the fighters being lost in a whirlwind of verbs and ambiguous pronouns. Like when cartoon characters fight, with only their flying fists visible outside the cloud of dust.

l.26 This line offers two translations of the same one word. 'Litchsore' may not be a very meaningful rendering to modern readers, but it's there for reasons of etymology. Litch / lych / lich is an archaic word for body and more specifically corpse – thus, we still have 'lichgates' – covered gates outside church yards – and of course the zombie 'Lich King' from World of Warcraft . . .

'Hurt in corpse' is my other translation of the same kenning, 'licsar'. I picked the word 'corpse' because it is less archaic than 'litch' but has undergone that same definition shift – from originally meaning any 'body' (as does 'corps' in French) to only meaning 'dead body'. This is unconsciously important since Grendel is, himself, also about to shift, more violently, from being a body to being a dead body.

The Zaqqum Tree II

l.24 The original doesn't make this simile explicit, but it's there to be enjoyed if one connects the dots. It's what my editor Don Paterson would call a poetic 'isologue': the righteous sit by fresh springs and gaze into beautiful eyes – the comparison is unavoidable, especially when you know there is a pun in the original – the Arabic word has the sense of both 'eye' and 'spring'.

ACKNOWLEDGEMENTS

An extended excerpt from this book was published in *Rialto 89* in 2017. Thanks to Michael Mackmin and Will Harris for allowing it so much space.

As well as editions of *Beowulf* by Klaeber and Jack, I have made full use of the resources available at Dr Benjamin Slade's 'Beowulf in Steoraume' website, www.heorot.dk

My translations of the Qur'ān made substantial use of Kais Dukes' Qur'ānic Arabic Corpus project, *corpus.quran.com*.

Many thanks to the following:
To Will Harris again, this time in his capacity as friend, collaborator, generous reader and truly great poet. His early help with these poems was foundational.

To Emmett and Matt for playing a very interesting game of Rock, Paper, Scissors. And to Rob, for being the stag on a stag night none of us will ever forget.

To Matthew Turner, for his patient and clear-headed advice on how to handle some of this book's sensitive material.

To Don Paterson, for being an intuitive reader, a perceptive and incisive editor, and for telling me to stop apologising so much in the notes.

To Andrew Zurcher, whose last-minute contribution to a difficult line in the poem *Rock, Paper, Scissors* borders on authorship.

To everyone at the Seamus Heaney Centre for Poetry at Queen's University Belfast, and Edna Longley particularly, for awarding my first book, *Useful Verses*, their first collection prize. The prize and the opportunities for work and travel it afforded were invaluable.

To the Poetry Society and everyone associated with the Foyle Young Poets of the Year Award. Without the award's shaping influence on me as a teen I wouldn't be writing now and neither would a whole tribe of my contemporaries.

To my wife, Jenny Daggett. The fact that I was able to finish a book during the year that followed the birth of our first child is entirely down to Jenny's generous emotional, intellectual and logistical support at a time when I had no business taking up such precious resources.

To my daughter, Ivy Daggett-Osmond, who is now much bigger than an avocado, but still not very big at all.